Garden Planner for 5 Years

5 Selectable Years of Garden Budgets, Garden Planings and Garden Logs

By David Brian

AF236247

Garden Planner for 5 Years

5 Selectable Years of Garden Budgets, Garden Planings and Garden Logs

David Brian

Administrator of https://redwormfarms.com

Bibliografische Information der Deutschen Nationalbibliothek:
Die Deutsche Nationalbibliothek verzeichnet diese Publikation in der Deutschen Nationalbibliografie; detaillierte bibliografische Daten sind im Internet über http://dnb.dnb.de abrufbar.

© 2021 David Brian

Herstellung und Verlag: BoD – Books on Demand, Norderstedt

ISBN: 978-3-7543-0422-8

My Garden Plan
By

_____

Years: _____ to _____

YEAR

_____

Gardening Projects

YEARLY GOALS

NEW PROJECTS

NEW TECHNIQUES

NOTES

Gardening TO DO LIST

CHORES/ERRANDS:

- [ ] _____
- [ ] _____
- [ ] _____
- [ ] _____
- [ ] _____
- [ ] _____
- [ ] _____
- [ ] _____
- [ ] _____
- [ ] _____
- [ ] _____
- [ ] _____
- [ ] _____
- [ ] _____
- [ ] _____
- [ ] _____
- [ ] _____

NOTES:

_____
_____
_____
_____
_____
_____
_____
_____
_____
_____
_____
_____
_____
_____

Gardening BUDGET

VEGETABLES/HERBS	AMOUNT
SUBTOTAL:	

FERTILIZER/MISC	AMOUNT
SUBTOTAL:	

FRUIT	AMOUNT
SUBTOTAL:	

FLOWERS	AMOUNT
SUBTOTAL:	

TOTALS	AMOUNT
TOTAL:	

SEEDLINGS *Log*

VARIETY	Indoor Start	Transplant On	Row	Harvested On

PLANTS *Log*

PLANT	Qty	Row	Planted On	Harvested On

Seed Packet INFO

CROP/ VARIETY	SOWING DEPTH	DAYS TO GERMINATE	DAYS TO MATURITY	HARVEST WINDOW

Planner (Sq. Ft_____) Each square is approximately___

PEST Control

BED/ROW	CROP/FAMILY	PEST	DISEASE	TREATMENT:

Monthly Harvest Calendar

MONTH:

MONTH:

MONTH:

MONTH:

MONTH:

MONTH:

MONTH:

MONTH:

MONTH:

Gardening Notes

Gardening Notes

Gardening Sketches

Gardening Sketches

YEAR

_____

Gardening Projects

YEARLY GOALS

NEW PROJECTS

NEW TECHNIQUES

NOTES

Gardening TO DO LIST

CHORES/ERRANDS: **NOTES:**

☐ _____   _____

☐ _____   _____

☐ _____   _____

☐ _____   _____

☐ _____   _____

☐ _____   _____

☐ _____   _____

☐ _____   _____

☐ _____   _____

☐ _____   _____

☐ _____   _____

☐ _____   _____

☐ _____   _____

☐ _____   _____

☐ _____   _____

☐ _____   _____

☐ _____   _____

Gardening BUDGET

VEGETABLES/HERBS	AMOUNT
SUBTOTAL:	

FERTILIZER/MISC	AMOUNT
SUBTOTAL:	

FRUIT	AMOUNT
SUBTOTAL:	

FLOWERS	AMOUNT
SUBTOTAL:	

TOTALS	AMOUNT
TOTAL:	

Seedlings Log

VARIETY	Indoor Start	Transplant On	Row	Harvested On

PLANTS *Log*

PLANT	Qty	Row	Planted On	Harvested On

Seed Packet INFO

CROP/ VARIETY	SOWING DEPTH	DAYS TO GERMINATE	DAYS TO MATURITY	HARVEST WINDOW

Planner (Sq. Ft_____) Each square is approximately___

PEST Control

BED/ROW	CROP/FAMILY	PEST	DISEASE	TREATMENT:

Monthly HARVEST CALENDAR

☐ MONTH:

☐ MONTH:

☐ MONTH:

☐ MONTH:

☐ MONTH:

☐ MONTH:

☐ MONTH:

☐ MONTH:

☐ MONTH:

Gardening Notes

Gardening Notes

Gardening Sketches

Gardening Sketches

YEAR

_____

Gardening Projects

YEARLY GOALS

_____

_____

_____

_____

NEW PROJECTS

_____

_____

_____

_____

NEW TECHNIQUES

_____

_____

_____

_____

NOTES

_____

_____

_____

_____

Gardening TO DO LIST

CHORES/ERRANDS:

NOTES:

- [ ] _____
- [ ] _____
- [ ] _____
- [ ] _____
- [ ] _____
- [ ] _____
- [ ] _____
- [ ] _____
- [ ] _____
- [ ] _____
- [ ] _____
- [ ] _____
- [ ] _____
- [ ] _____
- [ ] _____
- [ ] _____

Gardening BUDGET

VEGETABLES/HERBS	AMOUNT
SUBTOTAL:	

FRUIT	AMOUNT
SUBTOTAL:	

FLOWERS	AMOUNT
SUBTOTAL:	

FERTILIZER/MISC	AMOUNT
SUBTOTAL:	

TOTALS	AMOUNT
TOTAL:	

SEEDLINGS *Log*

VARIETY	Indoor Start	Transplant On	Row	Harvested On

PLANTS *Log*

PLANT	Qty	Row	Planted On	Harvested On

Seed Packet INFO

CROP/ VARIETY	SOWING DEPTH	DAYS TO GERMINATE	DAYS TO MATURITY	HARVEST WINDOW

Planner (Sq. Ft_____) Each square is approximately___

PEST *Control*

BED/ROW	CROP/FAMILY	PEST	DISEASE	TREATMENT:

Monthly Harvest Calendar

MONTH:

MONTH:

MONTH:

MONTH:

MONTH:

MONTH:

MONTH:

MONTH:

MONTH:

Gardening Notes

Gardening Notes

Gardening Sketches

Gardening Sketches

YEAR

_____

Gardening Projects

YEARLY GOALS

NEW PROJECTS

NEW TECHNIQUES

NOTES

Gardening TO DO LIST

CHORES/ERRANDS:

☐ _____

☐ _____

☐ _____

☐ _____

☐ _____

☐ _____

☐ _____

☐ _____

☐ _____

☐ _____

☐ _____

☐ _____

☐ _____

☐ _____

☐ _____

☐ _____

☐ _____

NOTES:

_____

_____

_____

_____

_____

_____

_____

_____

_____

_____

_____

_____

_____

_____

Gardening BUDGET

VEGETABLES/HERBS	AMOUNT
SUBTOTAL:	

FRUIT	AMOUNT
SUBTOTAL:	

FLOWERS	AMOUNT
SUBTOTAL:	

FERTILIZER/MISC	AMOUNT
SUBTOTAL:	

TOTALS	AMOUNT
TOTAL:	

SEEDLINGS *Log*

VARIETY	Indoor Start	Transplant On	Row	Harvested On

PLANTS *Log*

PLANT	Qty	Row	Planted On	Harvested On

Seed Packet INFO

CROP/ VARIETY	SOWING DEPTH	DAYS TO GERMINATE	DAYS TO MATURITY	HARVEST WINDOW

Planner (Sq. Ft_____) Each square is approximately___

PEST *Control*

BED/ROW	CROP/FAMILY	PEST	DISEASE	TREATMENT:

Monthly HARVEST CALENDAR

MONTH:	MONTH:	MONTH:
☐	☐	☐

MONTH:	MONTH:	MONTH:
☐	☐	☐

MONTH:	MONTH:	MONTH:
☐	☐	☐

_____

_____

_____

Gardening Notes

Gardening Notes

Gardening Sketches

Gardening Sketches

YEAR

_____

Gardening Projects

YEARLY GOALS

NEW PROJECTS

NEW TECHNIQUES

NOTES

Gardening TO DO LIST

CHORES/ERRANDS:

NOTES:

☐ _____

☐ _____

☐ _____

☐ _____

☐ _____

☐ _____

☐ _____

☐ _____

☐ _____

☐ _____

☐ _____

☐ _____

☐ _____

☐ _____

☐ _____

☐ _____

_____

_____

_____

_____

_____

_____

_____

_____

_____

_____

_____

_____

_____

_____

_____

_____

Gardening BUDGET

VEGETABLES/HERBS	AMOUNT
SUBTOTAL:	

FRUIT	AMOUNT
SUBTOTAL:	

FLOWERS	AMOUNT
SUBTOTAL:	

FERTILIZER/MISC	AMOUNT
SUBTOTAL:	

TOTALS	AMOUNT
TOTAL:	

SEEDLINGS *Log*

VARIETY	Indoor Start	Transplant On	Row	Harvested On

PLANTS *Log*

PLANT	Qty	Row	Planted On	Harvested On

Seed Packet INFO

CROP/ VARIETY	SOWING DEPTH	DAYS TO GERMINATE	DAYS TO MATURITY	HARVEST WINDOW

Planner (Sq. Ft_____) Each square is approximately___

PEST Control

BED/ROW	CROP/FAMILY	PEST	DISEASE	TREATMENT:

Monthly HARVEST CALENDAR

MONTH:

MONTH:

MONTH:

MONTH:

MONTH:

MONTH:

MONTH:

MONTH:

MONTH:

Gardening Notes

Gardening Notes

Gardening Sketches

Gardening Sketches